SPIKE : MASTERING THE KENDAMA

By The Void

Illustrated by Donald Grant
Published by Butterfingers Books

Copyright ©2010

ISBN 978-1-898591-21-4

Copyright ©2010 The Void & Donald Grant

All rights reserved

First published 2010
Reprinted 2012 2013

No part of this book may be
reproduced without the prior
permission of the publisher

ISBN 978-1-898591-21-4

Published by Butterfingers Books

Also by the same authors:
"Knees! Further adventures in kendama"
ISBN 978-1-898591-22-1

To Alice

CONTENTS

Introduction	5	Trick Variations	27
Anatomy	6	Bird	28
Grips & Stance	7	Body Catch	29
Big Cup	8	Slip-On-Stick	29
Other Cups	9	Slip Grip Special	30
Candle	10	Jumping Stick	31
Orbit	11	Earth Turn	32
Moshikame	12	Turnovers	33
Body Bounce	13	Moon Landing	34
Tap-back	14	Bamboo Horse	35
Trapeze Acrobats	15	Suicide Aeroplane	35
Spike!	16	Rotor Blade	37
Faster Than Gravity	17	Flying Top	38
Hanging Spike	18	Clifftop	39
Aeroplane	19	Wingwalker	40
Swing In	20	Stabbing Heaven	41
Around Japan	21	Scoop Spike	42
Around the World	22	Everest	43
Chops	23	Other styles	44
Gunslinger	24	Competitions	45
Lighthouse	25	Epilogue	46
1-Turn Lighthouse	26	Thanks	48

INTRODUCTION

"Ken Who...?" - Guy Heathcote

Centuries ago there was "Cup and Ball". Later, the French evolved it into "Bilboquet", but in the early twentieth century, the Japanese added two extra cups, and the "Kendama" was born. Literally meaning "Sword-ball", this deceptive little monster at first seems just a simple toy, but after a few minutes play, you realise that it's an exercise in concentration, persistence and... er... exercise!

Welcome to the wonderful world of kendama. Read on to find out exactly how to tame this wee beastie!

The Void - September 2010

ANATOMY

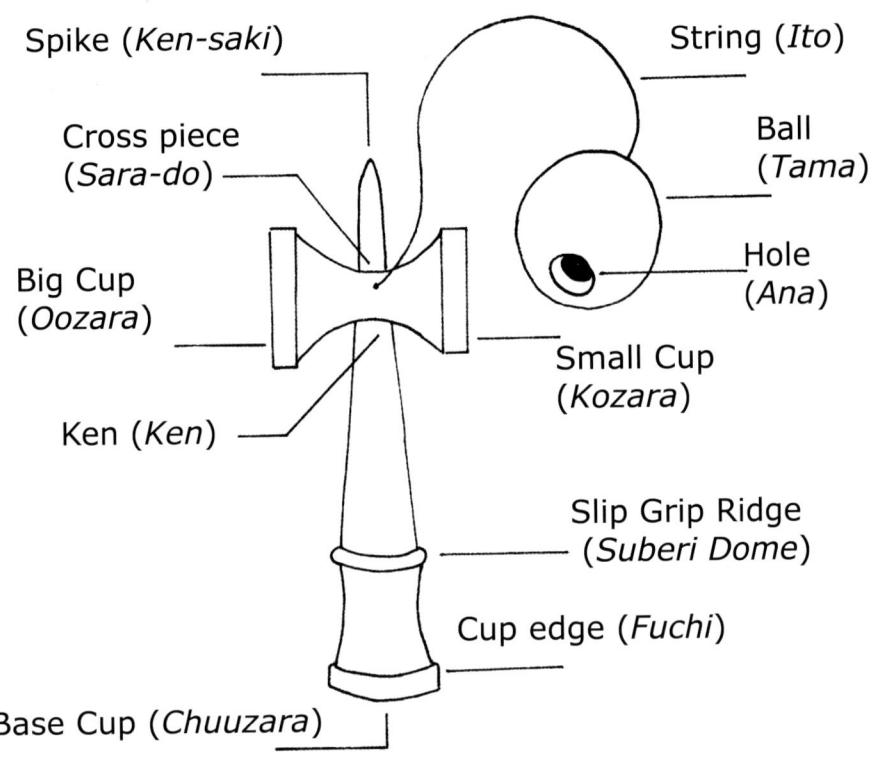

A typical kendama, strung left-handed.

GRIPS AND STANCE

Here are the grips you will need to know for the tricks in this book

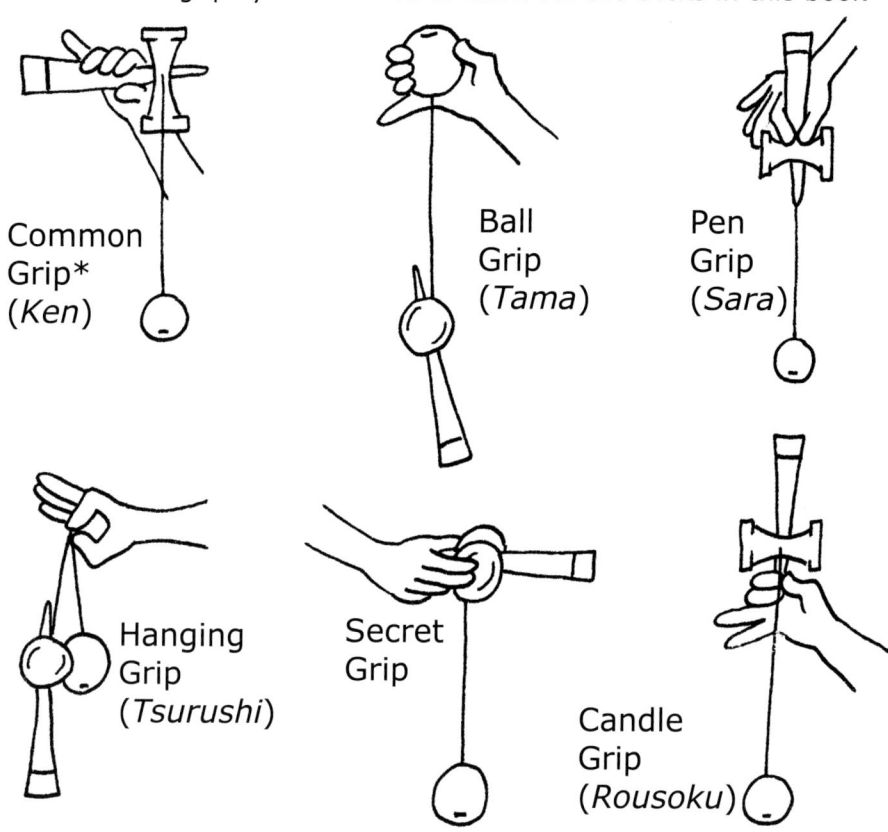

When playing kendama you should stand with your knees slightly bent and your feet about shoulder width apart. Your dominant foot should be placed a little forward of the other. It's important when playing kendama to use your entire body to make the pull up to catch, and because of this a proper stance can really improve your kendama play.

*Note for Lefties: When holding the ken in the Common grip, with the big cup facing you, the string should come out of the ken on the opposite side to your hand. You may need to re-string your kendama to achieve this.

Big Cup (Oozara / 大皿)

Grip used: Pen grip

Meet Spike.
He'll be your kendama guide throughout the book.

Start with your knees bent, and the ball hanging centrally. Straighten your legs sharply as you pull upwards to make the ball fly up to about chest height

As it rises, scoop the ken underneath and close to the ball, making sure the cross piece is vertical.

Bend your knees and lower your hand to make the catch.

Tip
Try to 'cushion' the catch, rather than letting the ball 'hit' the cup.

Small & Base Cups
(Kozara / 小皿 & Chuuzara / 中皿)

Grip used: Common grip or Pen grip

The technique for the next two tricks is exactly the same as for Big Cup, but the catches are slightly harder because the cups are smaller.

Small Cup, using Common grip

Base Cup, using Pen grip

A little more practice will be required, but if you remember to use your knees to soften the catches, they shouldn't be too hard!

Candle (Rousoku / ろうそく)

Grip used: Candle grip

This is essentially the same trick as Base Cup, but is slightly more difficult because of the different grip used. Concentrate on keeping the ken vertical.

Again, use the knees!

*Rejected book titles #4:
Kendama Nation*

Orbit (Tsubame Kaeshi / つばめ返し)

Grip used: Common grip

This trick gives you somewhere to go after you've made a catch. Start with Big Cup. Then throw the ball straight up, swirl the ken in a circle around the ball as it is flying up, and catch back in the big cup.

You can make the circle front to back, back to front, or sideways - as long as you fully 'orbit' the ball.

Variation
Try making an 'Orbit Launch' : "Big Cup", but with an orbit as you launch the ball upwards.

Moshi Kame (Moshi Kame / もしかめ)

Grip used: Pen grip

Start with Big Cup. Then throw the ball straight up, and rotate your forearm 90º so that the base cup is facing upwards.

Catch the ball on the base cup, then reverse the procedure to go back to big cup.

Straighten your legs for the throws, and bend your knees for the catches. (No, that's probably not the last use of the word 'knees' in this book!)

The official Japanese Kendama Association say that this trick should be performed at 135 catches per minute. You should probably start much slower than that while you're learning!

Body Bounce
(Rifutingu Oozara / リフティング大皿)

Grip used: Common grip or Pen grip

Pull up to cup, throw the ball, then bounce it off your knee/foot/forearm/etc before recatching in the cup.

How many bounces can you get in a row? How many different types of bounce?

Tip
Watch out for bony bits!
A ball on the funny bone isn't funny!

Tap-back (Maeuchi / 前打ち)

Grip used: Pen grip

Start with Big Cup.

Throw the ball straight up, and almost at the same time, rotate your forearm 90º. The base of the ken should gently tap the side of the ball as it is peaking.

Rotate the ken back again, to catch back in the big cup.

Tip
Don't tap too hard or the ball will fly off to the side!

Variation
Tap-on (Kajiya / かじ屋)
Keep rotating the ken in the same direction after the tap, and catch in the base cup.

Rejected book titles #12:
To The Lighthouse

Trapeze Acrobats
(Kuuchuu Buranko / 空中ブランコ)

Grip used: Loaded Ken, hanging grip

Put one or two fingers in the string loop, letting the loaded ken hang down. Swing the whole lot up and away from you, making two or three rotations. *Drive* the rotation with your finger, to stop the ball coming off the spike.

As the kendama is rising, remove your fingers from the loop, and the ball and the ken will separate. Catch the ken, let the ball swing down, but then quickly pull it back up again, and catch in the base cup.

Harder variation
If you can move your hand really quickly, you can make the catch without having to pull the ball up again.

Spike! (Tomeken / とめけん)

Grip used: Common grip

Here's where things really start to get fun. Start with the ball hanging between your knees, and sharply straighten your legs as you pull up. It is very important to make sure your upwards pull is directly along the line of the string, as any sideways motion will make the ball rotate as it rises, which makes the catch very difficult.

As the ball flies upwards, scoop the ken just underneath it, making sure you keep it completely vertical.

Rather than stabbing the ken upwards, just sink your knees and let the ball fall onto the spike.

Tip
Try to visualise the line of the string extending below the ball, and place the ken onto this imaginary line.

Faster Than Gravity
(Iai Tomeken / 居合いとめけん)

Grip used: Common grip

Raise your arm high, so the ball is hanging level with your face. Concentrate on the string hole at the top of the ball.

Now move FAST, pulling your hand down sharply to get the ken underneath the ball, and catch it on the spike.

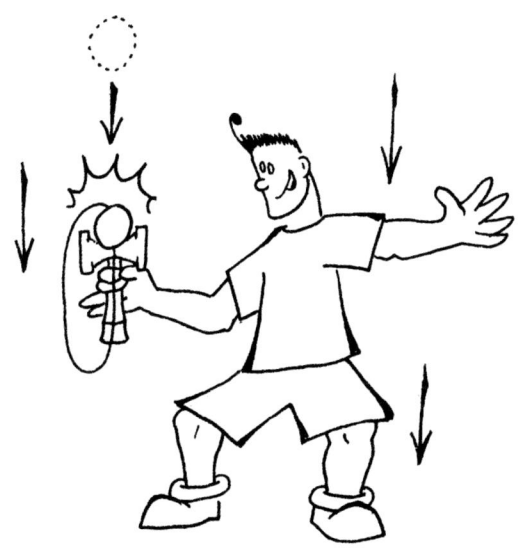

Tip
Going down into a crouch will give you a fraction of a second extra time.

17

Hanging Spike
(Tsurushi Tomeken / つるしとめけん)

Grip used: Hanging grip

The ball rests in the curve of the cross piece. The tip of the spike should always be above the ball.

Lift and throw the pinched string up, using your knees in the throw too.

Grab the ken while it is still moving upwards.

Swoop underneath the ball, for a triumphal spike catch!

Aeroplane (Hikouki / 飛行機)

Grip used: Ball grip

Start holding the ball a little away from your body, with the ken hanging down. Pull the ken back towards you so the string makes a 45º angle with the floor. Let go of the ken, and bend your knees...

...but then straighten them again immediately. The ken will fly up into the air, hopefully without too much spin.

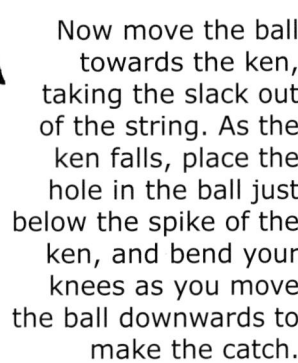

Now move the ball towards the ken, taking the slack out of the string. As the ken falls, place the hole in the ball just below the spike of the ken, and bend your knees as you move the ball downwards to make the catch.

Hard variation
Add an extra spin to the ken by giving a sharp tug when the string gets to horizontal. Or how about 2 extra spins?!

Swing In (Furiken / ふりけん)

Grip used: Common grip

This trick is Aeroplane, but upside down! Start in the Common grip, and with your other hand pull the ball back towards you. Sink your knees as you release, and straighten them again to get the ball to swing upwards.

As the string gets to horizontal, you will need to give a sharp tug backwards to make the ball rotate, otherwise the hole will stay facing away from you.

Release the tension on the string, then try to place the tip of the spike very close to the hole as it comes into view. Sink your hand and knees again, and let the ball fall onto the spike.

Tip
Think of the backwards tug as a reverse punch!

Around Japan (Nihon Isshuu / 日本一周)

Grip used: Common grip

Pull the ball up to catch in the small cup. Try to give a slight push forwards on launch, so that the hole is facing you. The ken should be positioned across your body for this catch.

Throw the ball up, and catch in the big cup. If the ball wasn't facing you after the first catch, try to use a little spin on this throw to turn it towards you. For this one, turn the ken so the spike faces forwards.

Throw the ball again, placing the tip of the spike by under the hole, and let the ball fall down onto the ken.

Tip
Hole control!

Around the World (Sekai Isshuu / 世界一周)
Grip used: Common grip

This trick is just like Around Japan, but there is an extra cup catch, in the base cup, before the spike catch.

Bring your elbow in towards your belly button for this extra catch. Keep the fingers straight and the wrist cocked.

Variations
Around The Village: Big Cup, then Spike
Around Prefecture: Base Cup, then Spike
Around Europe: Small Cup, Spike, Big Cup, Spike, Base Cup, Spike
Around the Cosmos: Side Spike catch, Spike, Small Cup, Spike, Big Cup, Spike, Base Cup, Spike. Phew!!
Around Tunbridge Wells: Don't ask!

Chops (Shutou Oozara / 手刀大皿)

Grip used: Pen grip

When trying cup tricks, try swiping your free hand between the ball and the ken.

Not too far, or you'll pull the ball off course by swiping into the string.

Try swiping in both directions, and if that's too easy, try an orbit swipe!

Gunslinger (Ganman / ガンマン)

Grip used: Modified Common grip

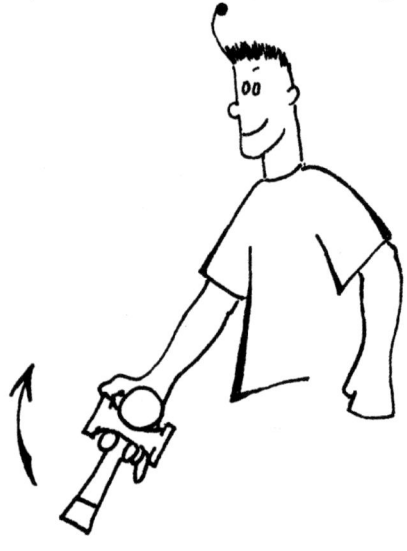

This is a trick that seems like it ought to be really easy, but has quite a knack to it. Hold the loaded ken with the ball resting in your palm, index finger under the small cup.

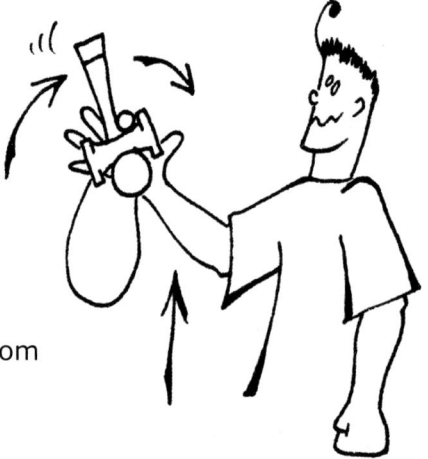

Swing the ken up away from you, releasing your grip entirely (apart from the index finger) as the shaft approaches horizontal.

Drive the ken around and downwards with your index finger, catching the shaft as it comes back down. The ball must stay on the spike the whole way around.

Tip
Imagine your finger tracing a shrinking spiral inwards - start slow and speed up.

Lighthouse (Toudai / 灯台)

Grip used: Ball grip

Start with straight legs, and dip down so that the ken almost touches the floor. Straighten the legs sharply as you pull up along the line of the string.

It should fly vertically upwards, so scoop the ball underneath it, close to the base cup, as the ken peaks.

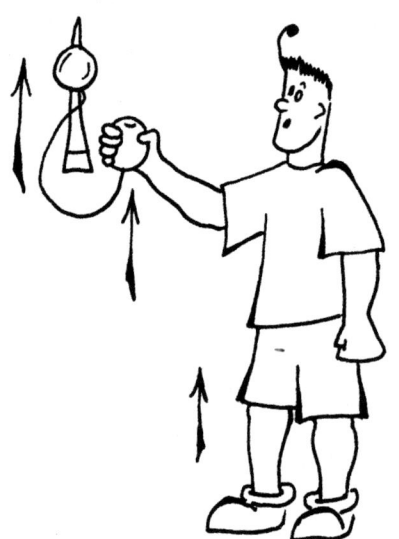

Let the ken drop onto the ball, sinking down with the hand and knees to soften the landing. If the balance is slightly off at this point, give a little upwards push to steady it.

Tip
Practise *just the balance* before you even try the trick - you won't be able to do one without the other! Keep your eyes on the tip of the spike.

Flashy exit
Falling Down (Saka otoshi / さか落とし)
Flip the balanced ken 180º to land the spike in the hole.

1-Turn Lighthouse
(Ikkaiten Toudai / 一回転灯台)

Grip used: Ball grip

Also known as 'Swing to Lighthouse'

Start with straight legs, pull the ken back towards you. As you release it, dip your knees and then straighten them again immediately.

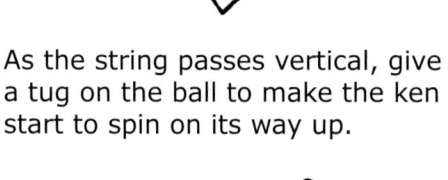

As the string passes vertical, give a tug on the ball to make the ken start to spin on its way up.

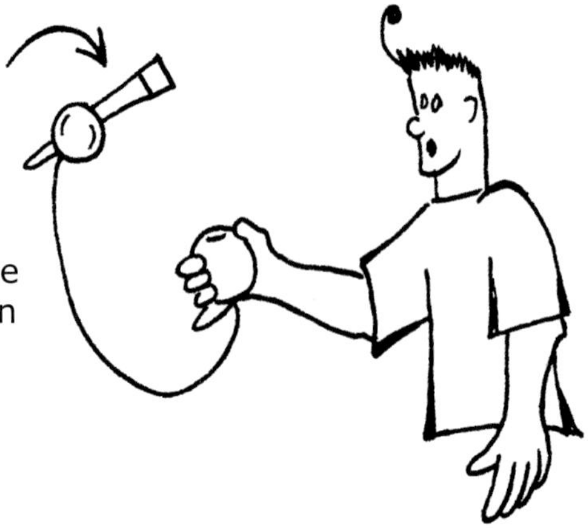

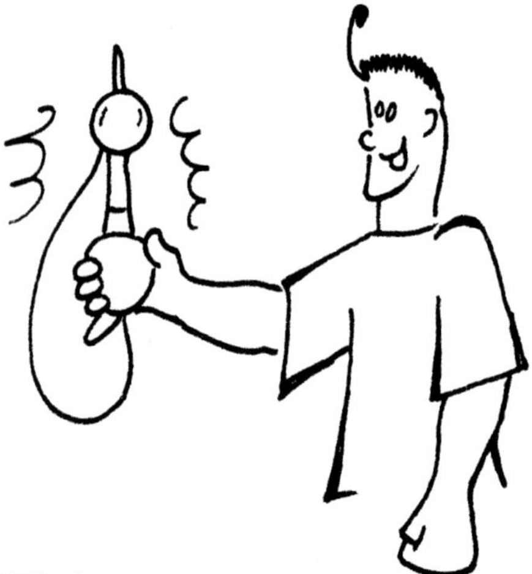

Try to keep your eyes on the base cup, and move the ball towards it as it comes into view, taking the slack off the string. Now all you need to do is make a miraculous catch into a balance! Yes, this is tough!

Tip
Try varying the amount of swing and tug until you get the feel of the trick.

Trick Variations

Grip used: All!

Let's pause for a breath here, and think about possible variations on kendama tricks. If you find yourself mastering all the tricks in this book*, and you want more challenges, just remember that each kendama trick can be done in at least 4 ways. Let's take the trick "Spike" as an example:

1) Straight up, as described on page 16
2) Swung in, (thus becoming "Swing in") as described on page 20
3) Hanging. Starting from the Hanging Grip, we get "Hanging Tomeken", as described on page 18.
4) Reverse! If you can swing away from you, you can also swing towards you (between your hand and your body). Much trickier.

What about "Faster than gravity" versions of other tricks too? Adding extra rotations? Transitioning between different tricks? Suicide versions? Once you begin to think about it, you'll see that there is no end to the number of tricks you can come up with.

Meanwhile....
Normal service will resume
on the next page!

A lesser-spotted unicorn

*Flippin' 'eck! Well done! ;-)

Bird (Uguisu / うぐいす)

Grip used: Common grip

Begin with the same launch as you do for Tomeken.

As you position the ken under the ball, make sure the edge of the big cup is horizontal. (The spike will be leaning away from you slightly).

Try to position the ken close to the ball just as it is peaking. Sink down a little *(use your knees! Have we mentioned the knees before? Will we mention them again....?)* to catch the ball leaning against the spike, with its hole resting on the edge of the big cup.

Tip
Practise the balance position on its own first. A small push upwards may help to steady the balance after the catch.

Hard Variation
Bird Over The Valley
(Uguisu No Taniwatari / うぐいすの谷渡り)
After making the catch for Bird, throw the ball up again a little, with no spin, quickly reposition the ken so that it leans towards you, and catch on the edge of the small cup. Then onto the spike.

Body Catch (Omikoshi / おみこし)

Grip used: Common grip

Pull up to catch the ball balanced on the side of the ken. The hole should be flat on the shaft, and the ball resting in the curve of the cross-piece.

Errr... that's it! :-)

Tip
Lots of cushioning to avoid wobble!

Slip-On-Stick (Kensaki Suberi / けん先すべり)

Grip used: Common grip

Pull up to catch the ball balanced on the side of the spike. The hole should be flat on the spike, and the ball resting in the curve of the cross piece.

From here, lift up as you pull the spike away from the ball by a couple of centimetres, but then quickly slide it back again, twisting upwards into the hole as you do so.

Tip
Keep the spike in contact with the ball at all times!

Bonus points for doing it Ninja-style!

Slip Grip Special
(Suberidome Gokui / すべり止め極意)

Grip used: Secret grip

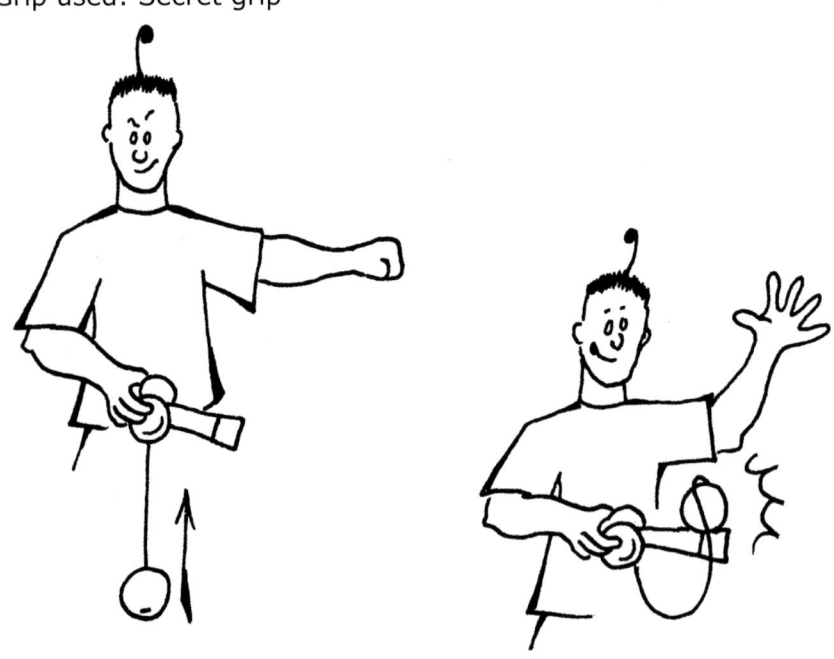

Start with the secret grip, with the upper side of the shaft horizontal. Pull straight up, move the ken so that the Slip Grip is under the ball hole, and catch in a balance. Catch the ball just after it has peaked.

Tip
Practise the balance position on its own first. A slight twist of the ken may save a wobbly catch.

Rejected book titles #17:
Twelve Angry Ken

Jumping Stick (Haneken / はねけん)

Grip used: Ball grip

Start with an Aeroplane.

Flick with your wrist to flip the ken up, out & around 360º. Use your knees to give height to the throw.

Keep your eyes on the tip of the spike, and catch it back in the hole.

Tip
Try both low fast flips and high slow ones, to see which you prefer.

Hard variations
Make a double spin!
Flip to Lighthouse instead.
Or flip to Moon Landing*? Eeek!

*Yes, I know you've flicked forwards to sneak a look at the really crazy stuff!

Earth Turn (Chikyuu Mawashi / 地球まわし)

Grip used: Common grip

Start with a Furiken.

Use your knees to throw the ball off the spike, and as you do so, give a quick push forwards with your hand, keeping the ken vertical.

The tip of the spike will send the ball into a spin as it takes off. Now sink your knees and catch the ball back on the spike.

Tip
Watch for the hole as it comes into view on the top of the ball.

Hard variation
Make a double spin!

Turnovers (Mochikaewaza / 持ちかえわざ)

Grip used: Common grip and Ball grip

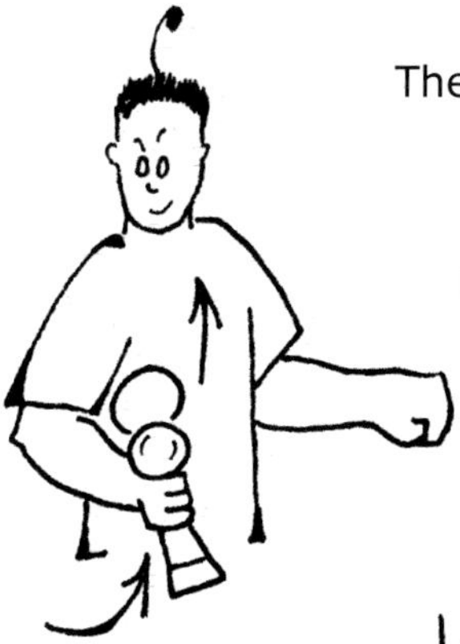

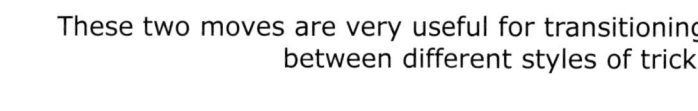

These two moves are very useful for transitioning between different styles of trick.

Holding a loaded ken, loft it into the air gently (use the knees) and let go. The ball should not leave the spike.

Quickly grab the ball, and swish it underneath the ken. You've just changed grips with an 'Apple Turnover'.

Now try reversing the process. Loft the kendama again, this time grabbing the ken and jamming it around in a semicircle.

That's a 'Jam Turnover'. Yes, we did have fun naming these tricks!

(Anyone else feeling peckish right now?)

Moon Landing
(Getsumen Chakuriku / 月面着陸)

Grip used: Ball grip *a.k.a. "Lunar Landing" or "Lunar"*

This trick requires a modified starting position.

Hook the string under the edge of the big cup, and let the ken hang freely like this.

Gently pull the ken backwards, so you are in a similar start position to Aeroplane. The release and launch are also just like Aeroplane.

For the catch, keep your eyes on the big cup, and use lots of cushioning.

Tip
Again, practise the balance first. It's more tilted than you might expect! Watch out for the ken hitting your thumb too.

Bamboo Horse (Takeuma / たけうま)

a.k.a. "Stilts"
Grip used: Ball grip

Start just as with Moon Landing. Allow the ken to rotate slightly more in the air, to catch as shown.

Yes, it is possible, but *really* hard!

Suicide Aeroplane (Uchuu Yuuei / 宇宙遊泳)

a.k.a. "Spacewalk"
Grip used: Common grip --> Ball grip

"Suicide" is a term borrowed from diabolo terminology, which means to let go of the prop entirely.

Start with the ken held in ken grip, spike pointing downwards, and the ball held in inverted ball grip. The string should be at 45 degrees to the ground, and across your body.

Release the ball so that it swings across your body, bending your knees as it does so. Now let the ball swing back again, straighten your legs, and release the ken entirely, sending the kendama spinning up into the air.

Keep your eyes on the ball. The kendama should spin exactly 360 degrees in the air.

When the string is horizontal, try to catch the ball, with your fingertips above the string, and your thumb below the string.

It's important not to touch the string at all.

Now bend your knees again as the ken swings under the ball and across your body, then quickly straighten them, which should help to stop the spin and lift the ken up nearly flat into the position for an aeroplane catch.

Tip
Remember, there are two knee dips on this one - one at the launch, and one between the two catches.

Rotor Blade (Yoko Haneken / 横はねけん)

a.k.a. "UFO"
Grip used: Ball grip

This is essentially the same trick as Jumping Stick, but in the horizontal plane.

Start holding the ken horizontally, string hole down, with the small cup facing you.

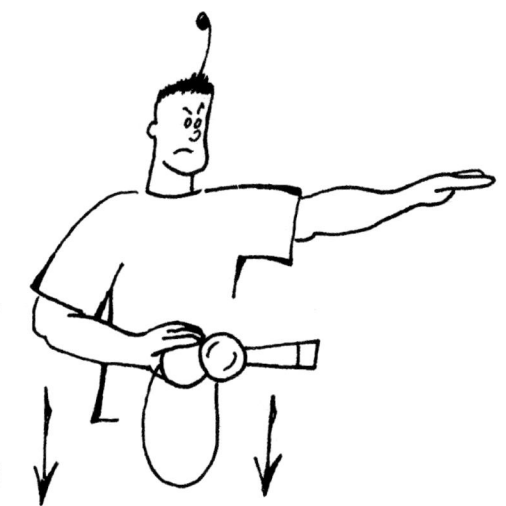

With two fingers on the top of the ball, and thumb beneath, give a push outwards at 45° to spin the ken out of the ball like a rotor blade.

Swish the ball onto the spike as it comes round, twisting your wrist upwards so that the ken doesn't fall out of the hole immediately.

Tip
Watch for the big cup to be facing you as the ken spins - that's the time to start the catching motion.

Flying Top (Take Tonbo / 竹とんぼ)

Grip used: Common grip

Start with a loaded kendama, and use your free hand to spin the ball as you throw it upwards.

Keeping your eyes on the hole, catch the ball straight back on the spike!

Tip
You can do this trick one handed, by using your thumb to give the spin.

Variation
Spinning Top (Koma/こま)

As above, but let the ball fall down to the bottom of the string, then pull up again to catch.

Clifftop (Chuuzara Gokui / 中皿極意)

Grip used: Secret grip (inverted)

Start with the secret grip, with the string hole uppermost, and the string dangling over the edge of the base cup.

Pull straight up, move the ken so that the edge of the base cup is under the ball hole, and catch in a balance. Catch the ball just after it has peaked.

Tip
More knees!
Any sideways movement of the hand during the launch will make the ball twist, so avoid that!

Now, did you notice the Tip there? I know it's a bit of a recurring theme, but anytime you are having trouble with getting a kendama trick, you can almost always guarantee that it's always the same problem. Yes, folks, the golden rule of kendama is....

MORE KNEES!

Wingwalker (Oozara Gokui / 大皿極意)

Grip used: Common grip

This trick is very similar to Bird, but without using the spike at all. A very steady hand is needed.

Hold the ken with the edge of the big cup horizontal, pull up to catch as in the picture.

[Author's note to illustrator: "Okay, Donald, I know that's a cop-out, but I don't have much more to say about it - it's just really hard!"]

Very Hard Variation
Wingrunner
Finish by transferring the ball to the equivalent balance on the small cup.

Rejected book titles #19, 21, 23, 7, 34, 38, 1, 11, 40, 31:

I Feel Like Clickin' Tonight
Kendama Full Force
Kendama Trix & Clix
Kendama Trick Frenzy
Little Book of Kendama
Team kd Langerz
Beyond our Ken
Kendamasphere!
Now That's What I Call Kendama
Instant Kendama

Stabbing Heaven
(Tama Tsukisashi / 玉つきさし)

Grip used: Pen grip

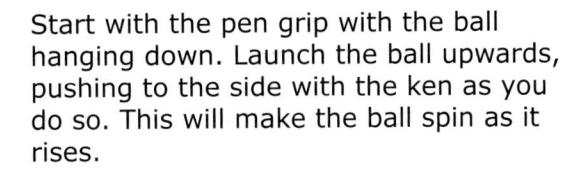

Start with the pen grip with the ball hanging down. Launch the ball upwards, pushing to the side with the ken as you do so. This will make the ball spin as it rises.

Once the ball has made a half-spin, and you can see the hole, stab the spike of the ken into the ball.

Of course, the ball is upside down, so to stop it falling straight off again, you have to swish the ken around 180º, in one fast sweeping motion.

Tip
Try forwards and sideways pushes during the launch. Both ways are possible - find your own style!

Scoop Spike (Sukuiken / すくいけん)

Grip used: Ball grip

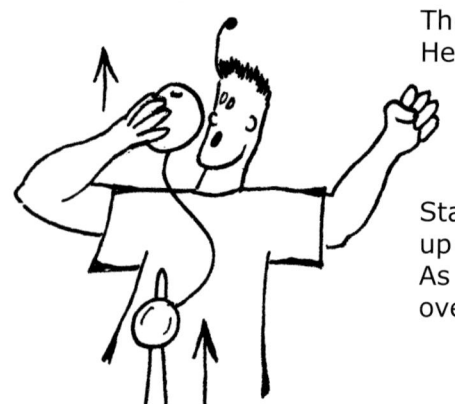

This is a similar trick to Stabbing Heaven, but with the ken inverted.

Start in the ball grip, and pull up as you would for Lighthouse. As the ken is rising, turn your hand over.

As the ken peaks, swoop the ball down onto the spike, turning your wrist as you do so, ending up in the same position as an aeroplane catch.

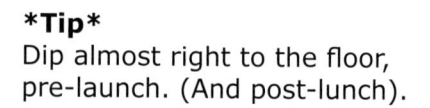

Tip
Dip almost right to the floor, pre-launch. (And post-lunch).

Everest (Eberesuto / エベレスト)

Grip used: Candle grip

Everest is a 3-stage trick.

Starting with the candle grip, pull the ball up to catch on the rim of the small cup, resting against the ken.

"Base Camp"

"Summit"

Next throw the ball up and catch on the base cup. It's best if you can do this with no added spin, as that will make the next stage much easier.

Now the really tricky bit! Throw the ball up again and catch on the rim of the far (big) cup.

Have fun figuring out where you can go from there!

"Descent"

43

OTHER STYLES OF PLAY

Stringless

The JKA allow you to use a stringless kendama to qualify the Moshikame tricks in their skill level tables. In his "Brief guide to the kendama", Guy Heathcote writes "Whilst this will obviously rule out Jump and Swing type tricks, a new set of juggling-related moves will make themselves available. In fact, for the jugglers amongst you, how about using two or even three balls with a single kendama body? Or tossing the ball between two people, each with a kendama body?" Or how about a ken in each hand with multiple balls?

Hydra

Invented by Robin Gunney, this involves two balls joined at either end of a string, and an unattached ken.

Extra ball(s?)

Another style we got from Robin. Add an extra, unstrung ball to a standard kendama, and see what kind of catches and switches you can come up with.

Rhythm

We credit this one to Yusuke Ito. You will no doubt have noticed the clicking sound made as the ball lands on the different cups.
But have you noticed that the different cups make different sounds? Try playing out a simple rhythm or a tune with your cup- and tap-clicks.

Tama-tama

For those who like their balances insanely difficult: Get a spare ball, and string it onto the string of a standard kendama, so that two balls hang down, one balanced on top of the other. Then try out your full repertoire of tricks with a VERY steady hand. And if you can keep that second ball balanced on top of the first, how about a Tama-tama-tama set-up?

COMPETITIONS

Both the British Kendama Association and the Japanese Kendama Association organise competitions. A couple of simple formats used by the BKA are as follows:

Trick Ladder
Draw up a list of tricks in ascending order of difficulty. Allow each player a number of attempts, say 3, at the first trick. If they succeed, they get to try the next trick in the list. The player who gets furthest up the list wins!

Speed Trick Challenge
Again, draw up a list of tricks. Players race against the clock or each other to do the tricks in order. Misses don't count, you just keep going until you get each trick. Here's the BKA STC list, to get you started. How fast can you complete it?

1. Oozara / Big cup
2. Kozara / Small cup
3. Chuuzara / Base cup
4. Rousoku / Candlestick
5. Swing to Oozara (String must remain taut until ball is above the level of the ken)
6. Tsubame Kaeshi / Orbit (Oozara>Orbit>Oozara)
7. Tomeken / Spike
8. Maeuchi / Tap-back (Oozara>tap ball with ken>Oozara)
9. Hikouki / Aeroplane
10. Moshi kame for 10 catches

Moshi kame endurance
Two or more players face off to see how long they can keep going at Moshikame. Ready? 3 - 2 - 1 - Go!

THE LAST WORD

Go on, admit it, the first time you saw a kendama, you thought there were just 4 tricks you could do with it, right? I hope this book has opened your eyes to the myriad possibilities that this simple little toy offers.

You're probably exhausted by now, and your knees no doubt need a rest, so why not take this chance to go and visit the British Kendama Association website at www.kendama.co.uk for more info?

See you at a competition?

Keep on Clicking!

The Void

THANK YOU....

Matt Hall - Partly for having the gall to actually *ask* for this book to be dedicated to him, partly for translations, but mostly for being the best inspiration a kendama newbie could ever want.

Donald - For suggesting the idea of a book in the first place, and for wonderful illustrations.

Laurie at Butterfingers Books - For the ISBN and lots of useful publishing tips. (Who knew there was so much to know about paper?!)

Harry Grant - For keeping an eye on our practices.

Guy, Robin & the rest of TeamKD - For getting the ball rolling, and supporting things en route.

David Marchant - For unparalleled zealotry in the kendama cause.

The JKA, Yusuke Ito, K.CIMA, and all the Japanese players - For inspiration, and showing us how far we have to go.

And all kendama players everywhere!

CLICK!